MW01706563

BIBLICAL PARTNERSHIP:

God's Way to Financial Increase

by

JERRY SAVELLE

SPECIAL DEDICATION

For those of you who are partners with this ministry, I dedicate this book to you in honor of your faithful support.

Your prayers and your contributions are enabling us to reach masses of people all over the world with the uncompromising Word of Faith.

May God richly bless you in every area of your lives.

In Him,

Dr. Jerry Savelle

Unless otherwise indicated, all
Scripture quotations are taken from
the *King James Version* of the Bible.

Biblical Partnership:
God's Way to Financial Increase
ISBN 0-9655352-5-8

P. O. Box 748
Crowley, TX 76036

Printed in the United States of America.

Biblical Partnership: God's Way to Financial Increase

How to Fulfill Your Vision

Do you have a dream in your heart that you feel God planted there? Can you see yourself walking in that dream? God has a purpose for each and every one of His children. He expects each of us to have a vision for our lives and to strive to fulfill that vision with everything that is within us.

So, what's the secret to fulfilling our vision? Obviously, prayer and seeking God's wisdom. But there's another secret to achieving the God-inspired plans for our lives that most of the Body of Christ has overlooked, and this is what I want to talk about in this little book.

One of the quickest ways to fulfill your vision is to help your "fathers in the faith" to fulfill their vision. *What?* You may be asking. It's true. The quickest way for you to achieve your goals in life is to help your instructors, your teachers in the faith, those who have made the greatest impact in your life, to achieve their goals.

I'm sure there are certain men and women who have made a powerful impact in your walk with God. It might be the one who encourages you when you're down. Every time you put his or her tape on, your faith gets energized and you're now ready to march after Satan and get back everything he has stolen from you.

It could be the minister who taught your family how to get out of debt. It could be the minister who encouraged you to get over your past and not feel ashamed and rejected anymore. A father in the faith is one who has instructed you, taught you, and helped you in your walk of faith and continually imparts into your life.

I've had many people impact my life and impart into me, but the three men who have been most influential in my life and ministry are: 1) Oral Roberts 2) Kenneth Copeland and 3) Kenneth Hagin. All three of these men have made tremendous impartation into my life. They are my mentors. They receive me and accept me as their equal, but to me they will always be my fathers in the faith. I listen to their tapes. I read their books. I read their magazines. I learn from them, and I honor and esteem them highly.

Now with all the instruction these men have imparted into my life, it would be a violation of spiritual law if I didn't support them. Don't close the book now just because I'm talking about financial support. Read on because what I'm about to share with you can change your life forever. I'm going to share something with you that I believe is very vital to the Body of Christ all over the world. I refer to it as the LAW OF RECIPROCITY. Now you may be saying, *What in the world did he just say?* This is a spiritual law that we see in the Word of God, and it's something that, by and large, the Body of Christ has very little knowledge of.

Webster's dictionary simply says *to reciprocate* means to give or to return in kind. For instance, if someone said, "Brother Jerry, I would like to buy your lunch today." So I go to lunch with him and he buys my lunch. And when I see him again, I say, "Remember when you bought me lunch the other day? Well, I'd like to take you to lunch today." That is reciprocation. What am I doing? I am giving or returning in kind.

I believe it's something that each and every one of us should have a revelation of. It's something that should be operative in our lives. If you're not doing it, then you're not enjoying the fullness of God. If you don't understand this law and you're not applying this law in your Christian life, then you will be limited as to how much of God's blessings you will enjoy.

If someone blesses your life, ministers to you frequently, invests into the growth of your spiritual life, then it's only right that you, in turn, sow back into his or her life as well.

The apostle Paul wrote in Romans 1:11, *For I long to see you, that I may impart unto you some spiritual gift . . .* Every true minister of God has the ability to impart a gift. I'm talking about someone who is anointed of God, called of God and walking in that anointing, then there will be something in their life that is transmittable. It can be imparted into others.

There's one word that comes to my mind when I think of Kenneth Hagin's ministry and that's the word "faith." And because of my association with Brother Hagin's ministry, through his teachings, his books, his meetings, I believe that the same faith that is in his ministry has come into my ministry. A spiritual gift was imparted.

When I think of Oral Roberts, I think of healing and miracles. And because of my association, that same anointing came into my ministry. When I think of Kenneth Copeland, I think of prosperity. His ministry has done more for the Body of Christ perhaps than any other ministry in the world in teaching the Body of Christ how to prosper. And because of his teachings and my association with his ministry, prosperity has come into my ministry.

So notice the three primary things that have been imparted into my ministry as a result of my support of their ministries: Faith, healing and prosperity. It would be a violation of spiritual law after all the faith that's come into my ministry, all the healing that has come into my ministry, and all the prosperity that has come into my ministry, for me to fail to support these ministries. Not only would it be a violation of spiritual law, but I would also cut myself off from those anointings.

I encourage you right now to seriously pray about who your "fathers in the faith" are. Who has made the greatest impact in your life? If you aren't supporting the ministries of your fathers in the faith, I strongly urge you to start now. Don't ever forget your fathers. Helping your fathers fulfill their vision will enable you to fulfill yours.

Share All Good Things With Your Teachers

Let him that is taught in the word communicate unto him that teacheth in all good things.

Galatians 6:6

The King James really doesn't do this verse justice because you can miss the real meaning here by using the word *communicate.* Most of the time when we use the word *communicate,* we think in terms of speech and talking. I'm communicating to you, but in the Amplified Bible it says it this way, *Let him who receives instruction in the Word [of God] share all good things with his teacher [contributing to his support].*

Do you listen to tapes? Do you read books? Is there a particular preacher that you enjoy listening to his tapes perhaps more than any other preacher? Are there certain preachers in whom you identify; that is, they really speak to your heart every time you hear them preach? If so, then don't ever forget the people who have helped you the most. Don't ever forget the ministries that have changed your life for the better.

Do you need a financial blessing in your life? There's only one way to get there. It's by obeying God's Word. Paul is saying that if you are being instructed, then you should reciprocate. You should support that ministry or ministries that are instructing you.

The returns or the harvest that you experience in your life will be determined by the contribution that you make to those that have helped you the most.

Our ministry, Jerry Savelle Ministries International, has birthed a lot of other ministries. There are men and women who are in the ministry today because of this ministry. Some worked with me, worked under me and then they launched out into their own ministries. Some never really worked with me, but I was their mentor through tapes and books. There are churches all over the world today that started as a result of our ministry. The sad thing is most of them do not support this ministry. And that's a violation of spiritual law.

The thought never occurs to me to stop supporting my fathers in the faith. I would never stop supporting them. Why? One of the major reasons why I am where I am today is because of the instruction I received from them.

How beautiful are the feet of them that preach the gospel of peace, and bring glad tidings of good things!

Romans 10:15

For me and my house, Oral Roberts, Kenneth Hagin, and Kenneth Copeland's feet will always be beautiful throughout eternity. Why? Because it's what they preached that changed my life forever. I will never stop supporting them.

How to Get God Involved in Your Finances

STEP #1: TITHING

God expects you to be a tither. That is not an option, it is a command of God. And if you're not doing it, I'm just going to be very up-front, honest, bold and frank with you today, you're rebellious. If you think you're going to talk God into blessing you when you won't even follow the general commands of

God, then you're just wasting your time . . . and God's too.

Everyone wants to be blessed. But there are principles or spiritual laws that determine blessings, and you've got to be obedient to those laws.

You're not going to get God involved in your finances if you're not even tithing yet. You say, "Well, Brother Jerry, I don't have very much money." I can't find anywhere in the Bible where it says, when you get up to a certain level financially, then start tithing. God expects you to tithe where you are. You say, "Well, I only have a little." Then tithe 10% of it. "Well, I can't." Then don't blame me if you have financial problems. If you're not going to obey God's Word, then there's nothing I can do for you, and there's nothing God can do for you.

"Well, we were told we don't have to tithe." Then you were told wrong. "Well, our church doesn't believe in tithing." Then I'd leave that church because you'll never prosper going to that church. You've got to start with tithing, but it doesn't end there, that's just the starting point.

Bring ye all the tithes into the storehouse, that there may be meat in mine house, and prove me now herewith, saith the Lord of hosts, if I will not open you the windows of heaven, and pour you out a blessing, that there shall not be room enough to receive it.

And I will rebuke the devourer for your sakes, and he shall not destroy the fruits of your ground; neither shall your vine cast her fruit before the time in the field, saith the Lord of hosts.

Malachi 3:10-11

You might be asking, "Well, where do I tithe?" God says bring the tithe into the storehouse. The storehouse is where you're fed. That's where you're receiving nourishment and spiritual food. That's where you're receiving revelation knowledge.

You cannot expect financial blessings if you're not a tither. So, if you're praying, "O God, bless me financially," and you're not tithing, then you're out of order. You can't expect help from God if you're not a tither. God's not trying to create something that's hard for you. What God's doing is creating something that will be hard on the devil. When you tithe, it's hard on the devil because now you've got this promise: God will personally rebuke him for your sake. God will keep him out of your finances.

STEP #2: OFFERINGS

The Bible talks about tithes **and offerings.** When you tithe, you haven't even touched your money yet. All you did is show God you can be trusted with His money. God says, *The tithe is Mine. It is Holy, bring it to Me.* So, when you tithe, then all you have shown God is you can be trusted with His money.

But when you give offerings over and above the tithe, then you've shown God you can be trusted with *your money.* When God knows you can be trusted with His money and you can be trusted with your money, then God will <u>increase</u> your money exceedingly.

The returns or the harvest that you experience in your life will be determined by the contributions you make to those who have helped you the most.

The most blessed Christians on this planet are those who help their instructors fulfill their vision. I know without a shadow of a doubt that I can trace the blessings of God on my life to the fact that for 30 years I have been a partner with my spiritual father, Kenneth Copeland. That's why I'm blessed. I have been contributing to his vision.

It all started when I first heard him preach the message that changed my life back in 1969. I didn't have any money. None. I had no money to contribute to him, but I wrote him a letter and I said, "Dear Brother Copeland, your teaching has absolutely revolutionized my life. If I had a thousand dollars (that was as big as I could think), I would give it to your ministry so that you could go all over America preaching to other Jerry Savelles like me who need to hear what you preach."

I said, "Sir, I don't have a thousand dollars. I don't even have a hundred dollars. I don't even have ten dollars. Sir, I don't even have one dollar I can send you." I said, "But I'm not without seed." This was in 1969 and God taught me this when I was less than three months old in the Lord. I wrote, "Sir, all I've got to sow into your ministry is my prayer time. I pledge and promise that I will get up every morning at 6:00 and spend the first hour of my day praying for your ministry.

That's all the seed I've got." And I did it faithfully.

That was all the seed I had. And do you know what happened? God honored that. There came a day when I was able to walk up to him and hand him a thousand dollars. Praise God. When I handed him that thousand dollars, I looked him in the eye and I said, "Sir, there will come a time when I'll give you ten thousand."

I walked away thinking, *Dear God, ten thousand!* But God honored that and there came a day when I walked up to him, and I handed him the check for ten thousand. What am I doing? I'm honoring my father. I'm honoring my instructors. I'm honoring those who have impacted my life the most. Consequently, I am a very blessed man.

Kenneth Copeland, Oral Roberts, and Kenneth Hagin know they can count on my support forever, and I attribute the blessings of God on my life to the fact that I have honored my fathers for 30 years. I will not forget them. I am what I am today because of the impartation they made in me when I was a nobody. When Jerry Savelle couldn't even get out of town, much less go to the world, they believed in me. They imparted into me. They taught me. Kenneth Copeland took me in like a son and raised me on the Gospel. I am not going to forget that man. I am not going to lay his vision aside just because I have my own vision.

Invest Into Your Fathers

For though ye have ten thousand instructors in Christ, yet have ye not many fathers: for in Christ Jesus I have begotten you through the gospel. Wherefore I beseech you, be ye followers of me.

1 Corinthians 4:15-16

You might hear ten thousand preachers, but not all of them will be your fathers. Well, how do you know a father? This is someone who has invested into your life over a long period of time and has faithfully instructed you in the Word of God.

There are many preachers who may have a lot of charisma. They may have a large crowd, but if they never sow spiritual truths into your life, then they're not your fathers. And yet, the Body of Christ, by and large, is more attracted to instructors than they are fathers. There is a greater attraction to the guy who comes in one time, stirs up a lot of excitement, and has a lot of charisma than there is to a father.

Brother Lester Sumerall told me years ago, "Everywhere you go, plant something. Leave something behind. If it's nothing but tapes and books, leave something behind so that the people can grow." That's wisdom.

For it is written in the law of Moses, Thou shalt not muzzle the mouth of the ox that treadeth out the corn. Doth God take care for oxen?

Or saith he it altogether for our sakes? For our sakes, no doubt, this is written: that he that ploweth should plow in hope; and that he that thresheth in hope should be partaker of his hope.

If we have sown unto you spiritual things, is it a great thing if we shall reap your carnal things?

1 Corinthians 9:9-11

The Amplified says verse 11 this way, *If we have sown [the seed of] spiritual good among you, [is it too] much if we reap from your material benefits?*

In other words, Paul is saying it is not unreasonable for me to ask you to sow back into my ministry, to reciprocate. I'm sowing spiritual things into your lives, now you sow material things (finances) back into this ministry. In reality, it's what you should do.

Verse 12 says, *If others be partakers of this power over you, are not we rather?* What does that mean? In other words, if you're going to support people that just come through but don't help in your discipleship, if you're going to sow into them, shouldn't we expect you to sow into us since we're the ones who first brought you the truth? We're the ones who are fathering you. The Amplified says, *If others share in this rightful claim upon you, do not we [have a still better and greater claim]?* But then Paul says in verse 12, *However, we have never exercised this right.*

The Amplified says, *We have never exercised this right, but we endure everything rather than put a hindrance in the way [of the spread] of the good news (the Gospel) of Christ.*

He's saying, the reason I've never exercised this right over you is because I didn't want to burden you. We have never asked you for anything. We've been willing to do all the sowing, but in reality, I'm entitled to expect you to sow back into my life's work.

If I keep doing all the sowing and you don't reciprocate, then you will always be limited. I won't be limited, but you will. So, if we have sown the seed of spiritual good, then it's not too much for me to ask of you to sow back in material things. Isn't that what Paul is saying?

Render therefore to all their dues: tribute to whom tribute is due; custom to whom custom; fear to whom fear; and honour to whom honour.

Romans 13:7

It is scriptural law to honor those in whom honor is due. God expects you to honor those who have labored the most, planted in your life the most and have made the greatest impact in your life. Honor those people. The law of reciprocity opens the door to greater blessings in your life.

When somebody does something good for you, turn around and do something good back to them. When somebody blesses you, bless them. When somebody says a kind word to you when you are discouraged, then, when they're discouraged, give back a kind word. That's the law of reciprocity.

I thank my God upon every remembrance of you, Always in every prayer of mine for you all making request with joy, For your fellowship in the gospel from the first day until now.

Philippians 1:3-5

This was a partner letter from Paul. These people were begotten through his ministry. They had received instruction from Paul over a long period of time.

[I thank my God] for your fellowship (your sympathetic cooperation and contributions and partnership) in advancing the good news (the Gospel) from the first day [you heard it] until now.

Philippians 1:5
The Amplified Bible

And you Philippians yourselves well know that in the early days of the Gospel ministry, when I left Macedonia, no church (assembly) entered into partnership with me . . .

Philippians 4:15
The Amplified Bible

That's a very sad scripture to me. Of all the churches Paul established and all the churches Paul imparted into, only this one was his partner.

Another sad verse is from the writings of the apostle Paul at his death. Just imagine for a moment, sitting under the ministry of the apostle Paul. This is the most powerful man in the Gospel of his day. This man wrote two-thirds of the New Testament. But at his death he makes this statement, *Only Luke is with me.* Everyone else had left him.

Where were all those people who were healed? Where were all those people who experienced miracles? Where were all those people who grew up and became strong in the Lord? Where were they? They thought just like the Body of Christ thinks today, *Preachers are a dime a dozen.* Show us the latest. Bring us the newest. Give us the one with the most charisma. What about your fathers? What about those who have invested the most?

These are serious things, folks, and if the Body of Christ doesn't wake up to this and get a revelation of it, they'll never experience the fullness of God's blessings. A revelation of this will move you into a realm of financial blessing that you have never experienced before when you honor those who have invested the most into your life.

But my God shall supply all your need according to his riches in glory by Christ Jesus.

Philippians 4:19

This verse isn't for just anybody. He was only saying this to those who had communicated with him in giving and receiving and were in partnership with him.

This verse is for every person who will do what those Philippians did. Honor your fathers. Honor the ones who have imparted the most into your life.

The quickest way for you to achieve your goals is to help your fathers achieve theirs. The quickest way for your vision to come to pass is to help your fathers fulfill their vision.

Biblical partnership will change your financial status and will bring you into a place of the greatest blessings you've ever known. Don't overlook this powerful truth from God's Word. Now that you've seen it, begin to practice it. Remember, it's the doer of the Word who is blessed in his or her deeds.

Has this Ministry helped you in your spiritual growth?

If so, why not prayerfully consider becoming a partner with JSMI?

(See details on next page)

DEAR FRIEND,

You can be a part of spreading the Gospel of Jesus Christ to the nations. How? By becoming a partner with JSMI! It is our desire to touch and change lives all over the world through the uncompromising Word of God, and you can help make the vision possible through prayer and monthly financial support.

We have made available this special Partnership Program in order to express our appreciation to our friends for standing by our side as we take the Gospel to the nations. I assure you that your investment will produce great benefits both in God's kingdom and in your personal life. Carolyn and I appreciate your interest in our Ministry and we ask that you prayerfully consider becoming a partner with us. Why should you become a partner with JSMI? Because we get results!

In Him,

Dr. Jerry Savelle

PARTNERSHIP BENEFITS

1. Discounts up to 40% on Jerry Savelle's teaching materials.

The Jerry Savelle Faith Library contains materials on over 100 different subjects and topics designed to help you become the most dynamic Christian that you can be.

Now you can save up to 40% while building your own complete Jerry Savelle Faith Library consisting of books, cassettes, and videos. Selected messages will be made available at specially discounted prices (which expire after 30 days, so be sure to take advantage of them during the designated time period).

2. Free subscription to "Adventures In Faith" magazine.

Each issue features articles by Jerry Savelle, highlights on the many outreaches of Jerry Savelle Ministries around the world and a variety of new materials by Jerry Savelle which are designed to enhance every aspect of your life. As an Adventures In Faith partner, you will receive this inspirational magazine **free of charge.**

3. **Personal letter from Jerry Savelle each month.**

Jerry Savelle's personal letters are always encouraging, uplifting, and filled with nuggets of truth that can help you reach **success** and **happiness** in your Christian life. Many who now receive these letters have said, "Every month it seems that Brother Jerry knows just what I need to overcome my problems. I always look forward to receiving his faith-building letters."

4. **Free books.**

Jerry Savelle has written many inspirational books. As an Adventures In Faith partner, you are entitled to **one free copy** of every new paperback book published (except foreign) by Jerry Savelle.

5. Personal prayer and counseling.

Because we know that you are faced with difficult situations from time to time, a special **Prayer and Counseling Department** has been established within our organization. This department is staffed by qualified individuals who are knowledgeable in the Word of God. Their job is to help you find the answers you need to become successful in every area of your life.

You may write your prayer requests or questions to our office, or you may call and ask for one of our Prayer Department representatives between the hours of 8:30 a.m. and 5:00 p.m. Monday - Friday(CST). As an Adventures In Faith partner, your requests will be handled quickly and efficiently.

For a complete list of tapes, videos and books by Jerry Savelle, write or call:

Jerry Savelle Ministries International
P. O. Box 748
Crowley, TX 76036
817/297-3155

Feel free to include your prayer requests and comments when you write.

Other Books by Jerry Savelle:

Take Charge of Your Financial Destiny

From Devastation To Restoration

Walking In Divine Favor

Turning Your Dreams Into Reality

Turning Your Adversity Into Victory

Honoring Your Heritage Of Faith

Don't Let Go Of Your Dreams

Faith Building Daily Devotionals

The Force Of Joy

If Satan Can't Steal Your Joy, He Can't Keep Your Goods

A Right Mental Attitude

The Nature Of Faith

The Established Heart

Sharing Jesus Effectively

How To Overcome Financial Famine

You're Somebody Special To God